BOOK

3

All-American Series

I0189948

The Big Parade

By Gene & Bobbie Carnell

© 2017 by innerQuest, an imprint of Chiron Publications. All rights reserved. No part of this publication may be reproduced, stored in a retrieval system, or transmitted, in any form by any means, electronic, mechanical, photocopying, recording, or otherwise, without the prior written permission of the publisher, Chiron Publications, 932 Hendersonville Road, Suite 104, Asheville, North Carolina 28803.

innerQuestBooks.com
ChironPublicatons.com

innerQuest is a book imprint of Chiron Publications
Edited by Jennifer Fitzgerald
Interior and cover design by Lisa Alford
Printed primarily in the United States of America.

If you are an organization wishing to buy bulk quantities of this book, please contact Chiron Publications at generalmanager@chironpublications.com

ISBN 978-1-63051-434-1 paperback

Library of Congress Cataloging-in-Publication Data Pending

Art courtesy of Freepik.com, Creative Commons, and the New York Public Library Digital Collection

Dedicated to the men and women of
our Armed Forces who serve around the world
protecting America — and making
it safe for us all!

All-American Series

Hi, guys! My name is Scooter.

I am a 12-year-old Toy Fox Terrier. My breed was one of the first circus performers because of our perky spirits and great balance. I live with Uncle Sam and Aunt Samantha.

I am Black Mountain, North Carolina's "TOP DOG" of 2014. I love people and parades! Aunt Samantha trained me and I am really smart. I walk on the treadmill, open and close cabinet doors and turn on my own electric heater. But I really love to sleep.

Uncle Sam built me several wooden, custom-made vehicles to ride in parades. I have a '57 Chevy Bel-Aire convertible, a camouflaged military jeep and an awesome red, white and blue firetruck with ladders and everything. This year I'll be in a big buckskin rocking horse on wheels for the parade. My fans will be cheering along the route, "Scooter, Scooter, the little dog that rocks!" How cool is that?

I hope we can meet sometime. Remember—be kind to animals. We all love you!

Scooter

IN 1788, PHILADELPHIA INTRODUCED
A "FEDERAL PROCESSION" AND
PARADES QUICKLY CAUGHT ON IN OTHER
PARTS OF THE COUNTRY AS WELL.

PA-RADE (PE-RAD) n. Spanish parada, place for the exercise of the troops or review of marching troops. Also an organized march for display; a public walk of persons promenading (marching), together.

Let Uncle Sam tell you about a very special event and some very nice folks we met in a small town in the Blue Ridge Mountains last year.

They were Ralph and Jennifer Fisher and their children, Sean, age 10, and Emily, around 8 years old.

They had just finished breakfast.

One of their favorite activities was eating out together, they said, where they could share their feelings as well as food.

It was during our favorite holiday, Independence Day, which you probably know better as "The Fourth of July." We're always very busy around that time of the year.

Mrs. Fisher said they were up early, bouncing around the house excitedly begging them to see the big parade they'd heard about for weeks. This was only their second parade and they were ready.

It was a beautiful, bright summer day and they were looking forward to getting balloons. Emily especially loved them.

F-i-n-a-l-l-y, the time came for them to leave.

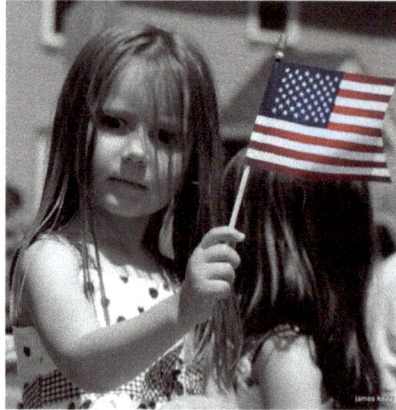

As they were loading up the van, they couldn't find Emily. They called and called and finally she came running out of the house, "We forgot our flags," she said holding up four little ones to wave.

The streets were lined with people, even though it was only 9 in the morning.

Must be a pretty big deal!

Their Dad let them out and went to park their vehicle. It seemed like everybody in town was there waiting for the parade to begin. They stopped first at the "staging" area.

Emily stopped Mrs. Weaver, her teacher from last year, and said, "Hi." Sean saw his buddies, Eli and Hector, and they talked about how good their Little League team was that year. They could "win-it-all."

Their Dad came back with the balloons he promised just as a gust of wind tore them from his hands. Disappointed, they all sat down on the curb on the blanket their Mom had brought for them.

And then sirens blared, drums boomed, and military men carrying the flag marched by. Instantly, they were all quiet and stood at attention with their hands over their hearts in reverent respect for the colors.

What a thrill it was!

HATS OFF!
ALONG THE STREET THERE COMES A
BLAZE OF BUGLES, A RUFFLE OF DRUMS
A FLASH OF COLOR BENEATH THE SKY;
HATS OFF!
THE FLAG IS PASSING BY!
–HENRY H. BENNETT

Then came pretty girls twirling their batons and young people dressed in snappy uniforms playing a stirring march.

Their Mom said it was called *The Stars and Stripes Forever* by John Phillip Sousa.

They said it made their feet want to fly and they could hardly stand still.

Next came the colorful floats, Emily's favorites.

There was one from the local American Legion with old veterans standing tall in their uniforms. She admitted she wasn't quite sure what that meant and planned to ask her father on the way home.

 "Oh look," she exclaimed.

Suddenly, Spangles the clown, came around the corner riding on a one-wheeled bicycle someone called a "unicycle." "How does he do that?" Emily wondered.

Maybe, when she learned to ride better, she could be in a parade like this on her bicycle.

Sean recognized the band from his middle school and saw Jimmy, their paperboy, playing his trumpet. "Boy, he's good," he told his Mom.

"Wow, look at those big beautiful horses pulling that last float, Daddy," Emily chirped. "And who is that elderly gentleman with the hat on? And that pretty lady in that old-fashion-looking dress?"

"That's Uncle Sam and Aunt Samantha," their Dad said. "I'd sure like to meet them. They're cool!" Sean exclaimed. Their Dad smiled to himself.

"Well, after the parade we'll go down to the square and talk with them," their Dad said. "Someone said there's going to be a big concert of patriotic music there later on."

As soon as the last float went by, the Fisher family fell in arm-in-arm, and in step with the music.

They were part of the parade—not just observers.

Being in the parade is much better than just watching.

After the concert was over they worked their way up to the stage to talk with the "marshals" as someone called them.

Dad introduced them all and Uncle Sam said, "I'm very glad to meet you Sean and Emily. Did you enjoy the parade?"

Emily looked closely at Uncle Sam. "He looks familiar," she thought. "Yes, we really did," she replied.

"Would you tell us why you and Aunt Samantha dress like that?"

"Surely, we want folks to know whose side we're on," Samantha laughed.

"And July 4th celebrates our independence from outside intervention or other people telling us what we should do. It reminds us of our liberties and privileges we dare not ever lose again," Uncle Sam said firmly. "In fact, one of our presidents named John Adams, who fought so long and hard for his vision of a new nation, said 'this day should be commemorated by solemn acts of devotion and gratitude.'"

"Yes, and with parades and Illuminations, too," Samantha added.

"I love fireworks, don't you, Sean? But that's for tonight. Are you all coming back for them?"

"Yeah!"

"Yeah!"

IN 1941, CONGRESS VOTED TO MAKE
THE FOURTH OF JULY – THE GREATEST
PATRIOTIC HOLIDAY IN THE U.S. –
A LEGAL FEDERAL HOLIDAY.

"You and your family and your neighbors are all partners-in-freedom. And those who went before you too. They paid the price and paved the way for us to enjoy all the benefits and blessings of being Americans."

"And so we could enjoy events like this in safety and comfort, too," Samantha said.

"These early heroes and patriots were willing to give of themselves and their resources so that everyone could feel included," Uncle Sam said. All this didn't just happen. It wasn't easy, but people who cared deeply about their families and friends were determined to make life better for everybody."

"Your family is strong too and you may grow up to be civic leaders like Mr. Woodard, your mayor and a good friend of ours. If you dream big enough, work hard, and make others' concerns just as important as your own, our country will always be strong and kind," Samantha counseled.

"You're right—we are all in this together," Uncle Sam said taking her hand.

"Okay, Uncle, you've got it," Sean said beaming. "Me too," Emily echoed as she stood tall and saluted. Their Mom and Dad were hugging Aunt Samantha as she and Sam waved and walked away.

WHAT A RECORD OF PATRIOTIC SERVICE PRESIDENT ADAMS' FAMILY HAD!

- ★ FATHER & SON, PRESIDENTS
- ★ GRANDSON, MINISTER TO ENGLAND
- ★ GREAT, GREAT GRANDSON, SECRETARY OF THE NAVY
- ★ SAMUEL ADAMS, ORGANIZER OF THE "BOSTON TEA PARTY"

Emily ran after them and said, "I just love the big eagle we see everywhere. Can you tell me about him?"

"We have promised to be at another ceremony in just a few minutes. But I'll write you a letter and tell you more about him. I want to let the readers know what happened to 'Victory' one time that caused us all some concern anyway, alright?" Uncle Sam said to Emily. "Alright! Goodbye for now!"

The eagle was named after the famous Victory medal
given to members of the army, navy and marines between
April 6, 1917 (when war was declared against Germany), and
November 11, 1918 (the date of the Armistice), halt of hostilities.

Armistice Day occurred on the 11th hours of the 11th day
of the 11th month. How about that?

On the way back home, they all kept reliving the wonderful morning they had enjoyed. Emily asked, "Have we seen that man somewhere before?" But no one responded.

By then it was lunch time so Mrs. Fisher suggested they stop at the drive-in for burgers and a shake. "Great!" they shouted. It was already a perfect day—with fireworks later that night!

Emily waited anxiously and watched for Uncle Sam's letter to arrive.

Sure enough, in just a few days, Miss Palermo, the postal lady, put it in the box by the street.

She could hardly wait to open it and ran in to get her Mom to help her read it.

Here's what it said:

Dear Sean and Emily,

How nice it was to meet you and your parents the other day. We're glad that you are interested in our country's past and the things that make us a strong united nation.

The great bold eagle is majestic and stately and a picture of dignity and grace. We choose the eagle because he soars above the clouds and best signifies the American spirit. Because of his courage, he's the central figure on the Great Seal of the United States. Perhaps you could be the marshals (honorary) citizen-leaders someday in a big parade like you saw in your town on July 4th. Everything is possible in the good old U.S.A. Or maybe on the committee that organizes one. And I hope you'll invite Samantha and me to come back and ride in it.

You have very nice parents and we enjoyed visiting with you after the parade. You do recall that we met you earlier at breakfast before, but we were out of uniform then.

Samantha says 'Hi' and encourages you both to work hard and get the best education possible. You'll need it to succeed in life. And stick together always, it's very important!

Love,

Uncle Sam

What is it that makes parades so special? Remember our definition at the front of this book says, "a parade is a line of marching soldiers."

But we Americans have improved on this to make it more gentle and pleasant. Now it is a happy occasion most of the time.

People are smiling and friendly. And everyone is going in the same direction. And, even though there are dozens of units in the parade, all of them are keeping together and cooperating.

Are there some lessons we can learn? You bet!

"I love a parade," don't you? They are great when people join together for a good time. Parades usually bring out the best in us—both the "walkers" and the "watchers."

Patriotic parades fill us with pride and purpose. These public displays, held up and down the streets of America every year, emphasize what's "right" about the U.S. They remind us that freedom is alive and well, and we are committed to preserving our way of life. Besides, they are great fun too!

Boys and girls, "tyrant" is a pleasant-sounding word but with an ugly meaning. To "tyrannize" someone means to bully them and demand of them unreasonable results. It shows a lack of respect and restraint and an unnatural love for their fellowman.

But I know that whatever you do when you get to the top of your profession, you will remember kindly the people you met along the way. Those who helped to boost you up the "ladder of success"—one step at a time!

And our parade is a great example of folks marching together "in step." Like our hearts, music has a beat and life has a rhythm. There is order and harmony in the ordinary, everyday experiences of life.

The Stars and Stripes Forever
(words and music by John Phillip Sousa)

Sousa, (1854 - 1932) U.S. band master and composer; he was the leader of the Marine Band in Washington before forming a world-touring band of his own.

Hurrah for the flag of the free–

May it wave as our standard forever,

The gem of the land and the sea,

The banner of the right!

Let despots remember the day

When our Fathers with mighty endeavors,

Proclaimed as they marched to the fray,

That by their might, and by their right,

It waves forever.

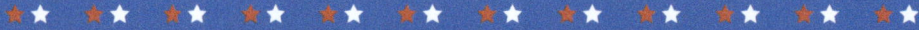

LESSONS FOR LIFE

1. It's hard to move forward if you are out-of-step with your neighbors—or classmates—or others.

2. Every puzzle piece must fit into its proper place to complete the picture. Everyone is important!

3. When we do these things, we enjoy ourselves more, and get more satisfaction out of life.

4. And then we make a clear statement about freedom and democracy. We offer a positive image to the world.

5. The "Fourth of July" reminds us not to be careless or take for granted the many privileges we have here.

www.ingramcontent.com/pod-product-compliance
Lightning Source LLC
Chambersburg PA
CBHW051310020426
42331CB00018B/3495